THERE, THERE

Cover photograph: Dorothea Lange; *Pulich* (from the Public defender series) A57.137.57124.2; Copyright the Dorothea Lange Collection, the Oakland Museum of California, City of Oakland. Gift of Paul S. Taylor

ISBN-13: 978-0615872148

WhiteViolet Press
24600 Mountain Avenue, 35
Hemet, California 92544

For Robin and Isabel

Acknowledgements

Many thanks to the editors of these magazines where many of these poems first appeared or will soon appear:

Aethlon: The Journal of Sports Literature: Tiger Stadium 1968
Alembic: He Led A Sheltered Life
Americas Review: The Book, A Daguerreotype of Renty Congo Slave, Notes
Argestes: Digging Weeds
Best American Poetry 2003: Villanelle
California Quarterly: Not Icarus
The Cape Rock: Aneurysm
Compass Rose: Cat Scan
Dislocate: The Stocking Cap
Eclipse: After Another Execution
Edgz: Tree Frog
88, A Journal of Contemporary Poetry: Mingus, Villanelle, Billy Higgins
Evergreen Review: It's Pretty Pathetic, He Tries, But It's Pretty Sad
Front Range Review: Sympathetic Nervous System
Fugue: Chops, Furred Cup
Grasslimb: Kilauea
G.W. Review: Somebody Threw a Big Rock Through The Window
The Healing Muse: Aneurysm
Hidden Oak: Pilgrimage
Higgs-Weldon: Rondeau
Inch: Triolet
The Kaleidoscope Review: Home Run
Limestone: Let Go
Lungfull: Free Write In Your Notebooks For Fifteen Minutes
Meridian Anthology of Contemporary Poetry: Lichen Planus
Nimrod International Journal: Reading Hayden's Frederick Douglass To The Dealers
Pennsylvania English: Family Album, The Tower of Skulls

Pleiades: A Raw Place Showing, Father and Son, George
   Abraham Higgins III
Plainsongs: No Particular Morning
Poetry East: Sea Turtle
Poetry Flash: Not Icarus
Quercus Review: Where You Lie
RiverSedge: Running with Isabel
SLAB: Kilauea, What Nationality Are You?
Southern Humanities Review: The Jewelry Box, Where You Lie
Salamander: Tornados
Spillway: After the Retinal Occlusion, I Was Born In,
Tidal Basin Review: Defending Sweet
Wisconsin Review: The Book of Life

Thanks to Robert Hayden, Richard Silberg and Mr. C. for starting
me off; to the following organizations for sustaining me along the
way, the Squaw Valley Community of Writers, the Community of
Writers at Warren Wilson College, the 13 Ways Workshop and
the Cave Canem Foundation; to the teachers and mentors who
generously gave of themselves, Ellen Bryant Voigt, Joan Aleshire,
Dan Tobin, Steve Orlen, Michael Harper, Carl Phillips, Toi Derri-
cotte, Cornelius Eady, Thomas Sayers Ellis, Terrance Hayes,
Angela Jackson, Elizabeth Alexander and Nikky Finney; to the
following friends and colleagues who spent many hours providing
feedback, consolation, criticism, good times, Rick Bursky, Roy
Jacobstein, Ian Wilson, Richard Gabriel, The YellowJackets,
Robert Thomas, Forrest Hamer, Dan Bellm, Rusty Morrison,
Charles and Gail Entrekin's writing group, David Watts, Joan Bar-
anow, fellow Cave Canem Fellows Gary Lilley, Chiyuma Elliott
and, of course, to my wife Sharon for letting me go and welcoming
me back.

THERE, THERE

George Higgins

White Violet Press

Table of Contents

I Was Born In   11
After Another Execution   12
After The Retinal Occlusion   13
Aneurysm   14
Base Line Three   15
The Book   16
The Book Of Life   17
Cat Scan   19
Chops   20
A Daguerreotype Of "Renty" A Congo Slave   21
Defending Sweet   22
Digging Weeds   24
Family Album   25
Father And Son   26
For Billy Higgins   27
Free Write In Your Notebooks For Fifteen Minutes   28
Furred Cup   29
George Abraham Higgins III   30
He Led A Sheltered Life   32
Home Run   33
It's Pretty Pathetic, He Tries, But It's Pretty Sad   34
Jesus Freaks   35
The Jewelry Box   36
The Kingdom Of Perpetual Night   37
Kilauea   38
Lady Bobcats   40
Let Go   41
Lichen Planus   42
Mingus   43
My Father   44

No Particular Morning   45
Not Icarus   46
Notes   47
Pilgrimage   48
A Raw Place Showing   49
Reading Hayden's Frederick Douglass To The Alleged Dealers   50
Rondeau   51
Running With Isabel   52
Sea Turtle   53
Somebody Threw A Big Rock Through The Window   54
The Stocking Cap   55
Sympathetic Nervous System   56
The Tao   57
Tiger Stadium 1968   58
Tornados   59
The Tower Of Skulls   60
Tree Frog   61
Triolet   62
Villanelle   63
What Nationality Are You   64
When I Heard About Troy Davis   65
Where You Lie   66

I Was Born In

a hospital in Motown I've never seen.
It's only been described to me by my nostalgic brother.
We were doing a drive by at dusk through the mean
streets of Detroit, feeling slightly smothered

by the environment, an urban moonscape
as alien to me then as Iraq is now.
We slowed down beside a fire escape
that was slightly rusted, horizontal, near a row

of houses where my hospital once stood.
The stair curled like an umbilical cord, a placenta
deposited and mummified, a fossil in the hood.
We tried to reconstruct the connective tissue. Huh?

Let me explain. I got a glimpse at my origins.
Or what was left of them when he took me for a spin.

After Another Execution

I read on a slip of paper at dinner tonight that
You must empty yourself before God may enter
so I emptied myself and found
the bottom of a lake bed
caked with sticky mud
next to a sign that said
do not swim.
Under a covering of mulch
the reflection of the stars
disappeared into the blackness.
I no longer want to reconcile myself to grief;
I'll sit with this thing tonight.
Let it crack the bowls, break the windows out.
I am weary of running away.

After The Retinal Occlusion

The microscopic pattern of a word
examined through a magnifying glass,
some specks of the O.E.D. clumped en masse.
My retina's become a page of floaters, blurred
and blue, starved by a clot of obscure
etymology. I look up morbidity, morass,
ruminate on recalcitrant, crepus-
cular, idiopathic, absurd.

I imagine my eye is adrift in a sea
of printer's ink or toner powder.
It's too late to paddle back to shore
so I settle in reluctantly.
The waves are becoming louder,
the words are promising something more.

Aneurysm

Seven hundred miles away one of the nurses ran a phone line to his
    bed:
I'm holding the receiver next to his ear. The docent in the Heard
    Museum tells us
about the ceramic bowls of the Mogollon, placed facedown
over the head of the deceased, sometimes in layers of four
as though they were *the dome of the sky and its four layers*,
each bowl pierced with a kill hole through which the soul ascends.

Base Line Three

Took one last shot in the empty field house
and dropped it through the threads. Still warm,
a fine coat of sweat on my arms, I palmed the ball
and fingered the pebbles on the leathery strips.

Gave it back to the African American in the cage
who before he handed me my ID asked:
Are you related to Earl Higgins, the NBA guard,
who played his high school ball in town?

I'm not I thought but said I was and who knows why?
And when I did I watched a look
cross the man's face.
He smiled and told me how much he loved to watch
my brother play. And I said: *I never could play much.*
Never you mind, he replied, handing me my card.

The Book

The man I will defend comes up at last
and sits behind the glass and smiles.
This prison has no outside window
wider than the human head. I look
into *The Book* to find his punishment
and show him where he fits.

The Book Of Life

And the woman said unto the serpent,
"We may eat of the fruit of the trees of the garden:
But of the fruit of the tree in the midst of the garden,
God hath said, 'Ye shall not eat it, lest ye die.'"

And the woman had enough sense to ignore the serpent
when he said, "Ye shall not surely die...ye shall be as
gods, knowing good and evil." She avoided eating
the fruit from the tree like the plague.

Instead, she spent her free time reading from
the book of life. Anonymously written,
the first and only chapter started out "In the beginning..."
followed by the serpent's interruption in which he

cataloged the material world surrounding Eve.
Beginning with the tree in the garden, he described
the branches that spread forth from the tree—
their color, density, texture, the leaves at their tips,

the veins in the leaves, the moisture within the veins,
the dew perspiring through the pores
and always with qualifications, amendments,
these descriptions went on endlessly.

The woman concentrated with such fervor
that she became unaware of the passage of time;
she became unaware of her own consciousness
as separate from the serpent or the tree or the sun.

At these times she was not thinking about the mechanics
of seeing the word symbols and translating them into images.
The words dissolved; eons passed; time conflated.
One hundred years felt like one second or a fraction of one

or ever increasingly smaller fractions of one
descending down Alice's tunnel or swirling like
one of those spinning tops with a coil painted on.
We forget she had no need to eat, have sex,

exercise, or raise children. Well, she did eat the fruit,
I'm sorry to say. My theory is that she simply forgot,
that it had been so long since she had spoken to the serpent,
that she lost the ability to distinguish between herself

and her surroundings. She was so unaware of her body
that she ate the fruit of the tree without knowing whether
she was reading or eating, without knowing
whether she was Eve, the serpent, the sun, or the dew.

Her eating was indistinguishable from her reading.
How could the book contain a narrative?
How could it contain a sinful act? Why would
she ever leave her perpetual waking dream?

Imagine her surprise when the Lord God said unto her,
"What is this that thou hast done?"

Cat Scan

The particulars are not important now—
the corner where the homicide occurred
comes perilously close to a row
of dingy apartments where the line is blurred
between the flats and hills between the blessed
and the condemned; the heroin was not
a character, it was a catalyst that messed
him up enough to make his every thought
pursue the goal of pleasure or relief.
I've read that money does the very same
thing, juices the brain and that for a brief
moment every synapse glows with celebrity—a fame
that can be turned on by any man
like a fold that's glowing in a scan.

Chops

I can barely play the melody to Doxy
despite five thousand dollars spent to learn
the fingerings, the embouchure, the orthodoxy

of technique that's so hard to master, no proxy
can perform it for you, mastery must be earned.
I can barely play the melody to Doxy

or intonate the nagging paradox
that: even with the lessons I can't discern
the fingerings, the embouchure, the orthodoxy

of a "natural." At least the Sonny Rollins boxed
set I bought will be on the shelf when I return.
I can barely play the melody to Doxy.

The phosphor ghosts inside the glowing box,
my sedative, distract me from this stern
admonishment: the fingerings, the embouchure, the orthodoxy

take all the time I haven't left. Hard knocks
not money are required, the days and nights already burned.
I can barely play the melody to Doxy
the fingerings, the embouchure, the orthodoxy.

A Daguerreotype Of "Renty" A Congo Slave

He owns the leaf in his hand, his owner's scorn.
The chemicals lop, etch, emulsify;
his gray hair radiates, a nest of thorns.

He stares back brutally, bleared, peppercorn,
some master's crop, crushed in the glare. His eyes
are silvery, oiled, almost metallic, toilworn.

Today, the cell mates clot below, most black.
In bright smocks, yellow and orange, they climb
the steps. How many behind the glass this week?

I pick a folder up from the ordered stack,
a criminal worn thin from serving time.
This one leans forward and begins to speak.

Defending Sweet

In 1925, Ossian Sweet, an African American physician, defended his newly-purchased home in a white neighborhood against a mob trying to force him out of his Garland Street address in Detroit, Michigan. Even though a white by-stander was shot and killed, Dr. Sweet and his family were eventually acquitted by an all-white jury of murder charges in what came to be known as the Sweet trials. At age six, Sweet witnessed the lynching of a neighbor, Fred Rochelle, who was set afire.

To be there at the beginning
That's the insufferable fantasy
In a clearing surrounded by fronds
A circle if you will is the arena
In which innocence is meticulously
Slaughtered in a ritual so common
The particulars of each variation
Need hardly be expressed but reside
In us like some unbidden voice
From some deep cellular memory
To first be able to recognize
And then be able to break that impulse
To desecrate the things we touch
As when Abraham took Isaac up to Moriah
For instance would blame the very heavens
We look up to the sky for an answer
For stage directions and hear only
The whisperings of the river Peace
Ossian Sweet to have been there
To have been there when Rochelle screamed
And fire curled around his legs
To have been there an hour before
And instead of allowing you to watch
To have walked you up the riverbed
To your parents' home
Through the thickets of flashy palms,
To have held you by the shoulder

And left you at their door
That would be defending
That would be my peculiar fantasy,
That is what I would call defending Sweet.

Digging Weeds

Forced out of the house
by the heat of argument.
The front yard, two small rectangles,
pocked with ragged weeds.
The weedy arms reach up
like empty baskets,
like a garden of hollow cabbage.
I kneel and poke
one tangled eye
of quarreling stems,
and press the metal tool
into the root and thrust.
Toppled skyward the weed
points, looking like
a shriveled torso in a hoop skirt.
I make a pile of them
by the front porch.
The grass thins.
Stray hairs. The mounds
of dry earth form where
weeds had been, and
I bend and remove them
one by one until my palm hurts
and again, and again
not stopping, moving past that point.

Family Album

You photograph the cans that overflow
with half-eaten pans of pizza and seagull excrement.
Crumpled cans of Surge and Mountain Dew
and glinting bands of Frito-Lay potato chips,
the standard meal.
You took the discarded fast food bags
and measured out the grams
of sugar, fat, cholesterol on your potter's scale,
once used for making glaze calculations.
Your project you've called it, the photos that you take
of smiling kids beside the rubbish they're waiting for the District
to pick up.
The children stand beside the marks scrawled on the walls:
Fuck the Bitches, murder, 187, 300s rule,
you label them inside a family album.
They're like the cobalt blues coming out of the kiln.
The thugs are running things you say.
The union can't get around to this
for months and months you say.

Father And Son

He held his son in his arms
that first week, when his son would sleep
against the curly bed
of his forearm's hair,
both sleeves rolled up.
He could see into the timpani,
the shell of the ear itself
a translucent blue veined cup.
"Newborn" He whispered.
Did the ear's membrane
flutter in unison
with his eyes, when those words,
left his mouth?

Was his son cradled in that tree,
just eleven years old,
before he fell?

He likes to imagine his son was day-dreaming.
It was after that when the seizures came,
and later the alcohol. And then he left.
He likes to think that there are people who care about his son still,
when he thinks of him at all, and that's not often.

Or that his son's body, even when his son is in some jail cell,
or on a county ward, or drying up in a concrete tank,
or just naked on a bed in a room,
can fold in upon itself
the way that newborn's ear
folded in upon itself
like a fist does where the thumb and first finger meet,
held up in self defense,
the startle reflex.

For Billy Higgins

After Philip Larkin

That cymbal you rake, sweeping and scuffing calls
like Pharoah "I want you to go to the brushes,"
and in my eyes your hi-hat never stalls

lifting up its pitch between the cadenced rush
of cocktail glasses, chatter, and scattered anecdotes,
your side men sitting down as though in prayer--

Yes, do that thing; please bend those notes!
While others dawdled, shifting in their chairs,
last night I watched you sitting just off stage

scatting the notes a week or two before you died.
I focused on your sallow face the program pages
crumpled in your hands, the swelling... I tried

to concentrate, to listen, to summon up the voice
I wished my father had. My stand-in, my name sake
creator, combining strokes with tenderness,

you conjured up the living breath, caressed
the sounds once more before the final take.

Free Write In Your Notebooks
For Fifteen Minutes

Monks invented vanity,
invented spirits raised from dead objects.

Jorge bent over the pew,
remembered his waist was
bent over the pew for days for monks.

Steady yourself,
note that memory shops
in the hippocampus with
its open wicker basket.
Memory retains a blouse, a skirt,
the yellow rug, a green chair, mirrors,
our static wardrobe from our closet.

Reflect on this.
You can construct ANYTHING.
You can write it in your notebook.
Now say hi to your tablet.
For less than the shirt off your back
you write: *a meteor rode over New Jersey.*

Furred Cup

How often does your sister write
an email note about your mother
who's been wandering at night
for hours lost a block away: another

incident. If she is mine it is the third
in just about a month. The suddenness
of change reminds me of a furred
surrealist cup, and the imaginary mess

I fantasize could now coagulate
inside its tangible abstraction.
The beaver pelt the artist glued and cut,
the follicles of hair are lots of fun,

except for the thing that's skinned, astray
and wandering only a block away.

George Abraham Higgins III

Henry James never liked being called junior.
It makes you instantly derivative, a sequel.
The III is hard for a six year old to write without a slant.
On the page does the III look like a pair of windows? A top hat?
More like prison bars.
Though there is something grandiose about it.
It's like the uniform of a Ugandan dictator.
Marcus Garvey would be proud to wear my name.
Those were the days before the III had been trumped by an X.
An advantage is, it's so theatrical, it slips on and off.
But what if you...
You might wear it to the grocery store.
You might wear it in the shower.
You might wear it while you're making love.
The III was lost at 16
although it continued to surface
on graduation presents, wedding gifts.
The loss of Abraham was foreseen and could be justified
as a time-saving measure, a concession to efficiency
no one could protest since it was being replaced with a stately A,
    period.
That's the way it stayed until my father died two years ago.
That's when the A, period was eliminated as well.
My wife said that if we had a boy I had a choice
he could be George Higgins IV or circumcised, but not both.
Only, George Wentworth Higgins II would be more Episcopalian.
Abraham Higgins more Hebraic.
George Higgins II, Esq. would barely fit on a business card.
I've through of changing it altogether to
G. Abraham Higgins if I wrote a legal thriller.
A simple G. A. Higgins would suggest T.S. Eliot or W.S. Merwin.
George Abraham Higgins unfortunately doesn't scan like William
Carlos Williams.

Perhaps I could change it to G.H. a near inversion of H.D.
I tried my mother's maiden name, Taylor Higgins.
A colleague said it sounded like the pen-name of a romance
    novelist.
In the end, I keep coming back to George Higgins
as plain as Henry James, who did what he could,
who worked in the dark and the rest, well.

He Led A Sheltered Life

You remind me that
I've overstayed my welcome.
You remind me that
summer evaporates,
that it amounts to no more than
a series of umbrella-covered chairs in Paris.

Step outside underneath a rainstorm
you say.
So I did.
Look, they all die in time
you say.
Slick images on TV die
you say.
Cesar Vallejo dies
you say.

With control and proportion I replied
It was condescension,
your depiction of where I was.
I've been outside before.
I made a debate smile, said
What do rain showers have to do with summer?
Water drummed on the sidewalk,
on the trees, raw missiles, raw sounds.
Water drummed on the car.
Please let me in now.

Home Run

"Perfect contact," he said almost dreamily.
"There's no sweeter feeling.
It's a feeling in my hands that I can't explain.
Something real soft.
You don't feel nothing but making a good sound."

It's Pretty Pathetic, He Tries,
But It's Pretty Sad

My indecision blinks
like a metronome.
Holy Rollers glisten in the spotlights.
I need more time to sell myself on religion.
Can Holy Rollers prove why
chromatic octaves rolled over Elvin Jones at the Blue Note?
He sounded cymbals,
music of the spheres,
out into table top light
while sad servers,
beached in the kitchen,
like fire flies,
rapped rough scales.
Look, I tried to swim the Channel once.
I swam, rotated, looked, turned.
Thirsty Channel you were on, remember?
I reflected:
I tries to has, yes I do.

Jesus Freaks

We stood in line for him,
under the purple glow of halogens,
a group of teenagers, cherubim,
and waited for the healing to begin.

Under the purple glow of halogens,
we bought our passage at the ticket booth
and waited for the healing to begin
in the auditorium, up on the stage of youth.

We bought our passage at the ticket booth
and took our seats in air-conditioned rows
in the auditorium, up on the stage of youth,
and waited for the Holy undertow

to drag us from our seats in air-conditioned rows.
We stood before the preacher in the polyester suit
and waited for the Holy undertow
to heal the lame and destitute.

Before the preacher in the polyester suit,
our own complaints diminished, atrophied,
when we saw him heal the lame and destitute,
whose faith was equal to their need.

Our own complaints diminished, atrophied,
we fell back with relief into the waiting limbs
of brethren and those whose faith was equal to their need.
We stood in line for him.

The Jewelry Box

A woman paints a scene on a wooden box
of two cats, two children,
herself, and a sliver of moon.
The forms float in a cobalt fluidity,
blackened but still rendered blue,
worked into the wooden box,
surrounded by burning stars,
silver hieroglyphics, ellipses.
The figures reach out
as if swimming in a dream
to touch one another's hand,
each leading the other forward silently.
One, a baby, looks to the mother
and she to the girl, all three naked,
all aware of their choreographed dance
in an oval of space,
in their own unspecified mythology.

The Kingdom Of Perpetual Night

Why is it that I am afraid to meet perpetual night?
Is it because I wish I could delete perpetual night?

Computer tablets glow like fireflies above the Spanish moss.
These paper lanterns temporarily defeat perpetual night.

Petroleum lights up the planet in its carbon glow.
How long will we force you into retreat perpetual night?

Around the axis of the world the spinning globe
Abandons daylight just in time to greet perpetual night.

An actor turns his face out to the audience
That's veiled behind a sheet of perpetual night.

I look into your eyes and see them staring back.
Your pupils can't compete with perpetual night.

Before long, George, it will be time to go to bed
Don't ever think that you can cheat perpetual night.

Kilauea

She led me down a crooked stair
to the dank entrance and
held my hand while

we walked through the center
of a dead flow, walls tinctured
with green lights. Someone read

that the surface hardened
while its core burned hot.
I imagined the black glass knuckles

overhead, a fist of plowed furrows.
Though I couldn't see its end
my eyes followed the trace

of wires roped from light to light
clipped up above the pitted floor.
You came to a stop; I watched

your face turn green and then dark
as you examined the curved walls.
Did we stop to take photographs,

sit our baby down,
her knee covered with ash?
Or was something lost,

Robin's tortoiseshell barrette
fidgeted through her fingers?
I cannot now remember.

I only know that we stopped
and then something triggered this fear in me
like the opening of a shutter's eye.

When I walked down to the beach
of black sand with you,
we watched the snow-like plume

of poisoned steam dissolve into the mist
that rose and fell above us like a fine net.
The pent-up gas flew from the sea.

Lady Bobcats

O, beautiful, O, graceful.

I've never seen anything like
this huddle. They have
more swagger than their mothers.

All the wet, damp winter,
on the break, the three man weave,
my daughter, sixth grader,
plays in her urban gym,
city games, the games
they play in Oakland.

Tonya, the coach,
says:

"Be aggressive."

"Stay down."

The moon also sets in Oakland,
and the Pleiades.

And so many city people
together there on the wooden bleachers.

Let Go

I take her to the park to have a little fun
and when she asks I decide that I might
as well give in, and permit her to let *her* kite
go. And then what? No matter how she runs

she can't catch up. And her plastic spool just guns
across the grass, the reservoir, and out of sight.
The jittery frame, abandoned, fights
the air, becomes a vague reflection in the sun.

What follows is our walk across the berm,
the blessedness of knowing that she's lost
herself in momentary clarity.
We also observe that what we've done has cost
us a trip to find the string, the tail we
think are lost. What's missing here we can't confirm.

Lichen Planus

My dentist incorrectly declared today, first day of spring,
when he checked my gums. Lichen is a crusty, scaly growth
found on rocks or trunks, a fungus class, ascomycetes.
And planus, level, flat. My latin teacher told me
it's possible to translate the legal term "habeas corpus"
without knowing what it means. Still there was some magic
in this not knowing. I loved to classify. In Botany I accumulated
the names: Sequoia sempervirens, Pseudotsuga
taxifolia, Quercus alba. Like newly minted bills they were
something tangible I could exchange for status
like a grade or a tactile metaphysics,
the regulated patterns of ferns behind the waxy
paper in the books from the arboretum.   My wife was pleased to hear about ⎯⎯⎯
my diagnosis she looked it up in our Mayo
Clinic book folding out the color plates. *It doesn't look so bad.*

Mingus

Everyone crowds the makeshift bandstand:
the younger couples dance
anywhere, squeeze forward
like a cheap special effect in a 50's Sci Fi flick,
and demonstrate detachment like a bag of tacks, the devil's cold
    fingers,
or saturation like smeared ink from a love letter.
A couple adjusts their Monet's "Waterlillies" umbrella,
so they can observe their younger reflections.
Beads of water falling over the tarp,
the condensation rising
with the recycled roots, chords and tonics,
mingling among us this afternoon.

My Father

bought a drink for Billie Holiday:
a scotch and milk. No way to verify
of course. I thought this harmless brag a lie.
Was just the thing a father might say
to a son some forty years later. But the way
he said it with a stab of condescension I
couldn't help but notice made me wonder why
he told me this. Was it meant to convey
a class distinction or ingratiate
himself to me? Was he trying to correct
a mis-impression of mine he couldn't name?
The smoky clubs, the smack, the booze, the late
Ms. Holiday indulged meant I should protect
my heart. I hear: *I'll never be the same.*

No Particular Morning

The angry man whose file I couldn't find,
the mother I offended when I didn't talk
to her, the man with golden teeth, their grind-
ing sound, the phone's continual squawk,
the broken metal hinge, one demented in-
mate in a holding cell I haven't seen
or someone who forgot exactly when
she was supposed to come to court, the mean-
ness of excuse, abuse and don't forget:
the knife that stuck inside the tattered screen,
the lady who he dragged across the street,
the purse he didn't get, the cell she didn't take,
the shrimp she stuffed inside her pants, the steak.

Not Icarus

This was not as when Icarus fell
There was no hubris.
The Marines were strapped face forward,
looking through the hatch.
The pilot worked the controls with precision,
but nonetheless the blade uncoupled
with a great whack
as when a fan belt breaks loose.

Afterwards, the ocean was
as flat and lusterless as mercury.
A lava lamp, fantastically slow.

I remembered these dead
when I saw the anemone
undulating and opening their senseless,
sensitive mouths.
They were rippling in the tide pools.

They were cool to eventuality, opportunists,
insensate.
Also luscious,
brilliant in color,
mute, rhythmic, living.

Notes

The young public defender,
feeling slightly dizzy, hands cold,
stares at his image
in the ridged metal closing on
the jail's elevator doors. Had a fight
with his wife that morning.
Remembered the seamless closing
of her angled jaw repeated now,
as was her silence, except now
the whirring motors overhead which last
until he reaches his floor, and sits
on the metal stool
between a window and a door,
and spreads his papers out.
The young mulatto, in wrist,
and ankle chains, escorted from below,
slumps against the facing door,
accordion folder between his fingers.
The contents spill, as though
a sac has been slit:
an occluded bag, rounded pencil stubs,
crumpled paper, requisition forms.
They wait and when the guards leave
they pick up those things.
For the first time the lawyer really looks at them,
the notes, on the lined, school boy paper
written in pencil in a careful hand.
The lawyer doesn't need them
but holds them in his arms.

Pilgrimage

When I was young
I'd paddle out
in the drunken canoe,
and toss the paddles overboard
and lie down on my back,
by myself dangling my hands.
The sea was a warm bath
dark as Communion wine.
On the shore,
a stone chapel lit by a single lamp.
Oarless, my canoe
had no rigging, no compass.
And through the sides
I'd hear the liquid lapping:
"No destination sought"
and hear the stars cry back
in their clear, precise and navigable voices:
"We have no patterns."

A Raw Place Showing

She left me all alone and went to church.
I know her faith is dangerous and so is God's.
In Eden, too, His forbidden fruit
hung dangling there like so many drops of mother's milk.
Mangoes, apricots, and plantains
bronzed in the sun. I know they say
He gave those two enough. The stern rewards
of husband and wife, the epiphanies we pick up
like crumbs wrung from work
were showered on their heads. In the Garden,
the tree was tainted by an oil
beneath the skin, with the snake God
put there to tell her she didn't have enough.
But I digress, of course, I put the needle in my vein
just after she was gone, tired of her taunts
and her distrust. Whatever grew inside me
was not in the poppy
but came from her hectoring distrust: "Don't do it," she said
and left. When our infant cried
I poked him in the ribs
to pay her back, or Him. It wasn't until the crying stopped
and I peeled off his clothes that I could see
the bruises bloom beneath his skin
too late to drop the fruit.

Reading Hayden's Frederick Douglass To The Alleged Dealers

Like attaching safety pins on baby diapers
I tie a Windsor knot over the alleged drug dealer's shoulder.
The brightly colored Salvation Army ties
I bought in bulk before my lecture
flutter like big box kites at Cesar Chavez Park
around their muscled necks.

Twelve recently arrested, said to be street dealers,
eighteen to twenty-one,
sit around the conference table at Probation Hall,
executives in their orange molded plastic chairs.
I try to mentor them by measuring their necks
and arms; I teach them how to iron shirts.

My auntie showed me how says one.
She flicks the water from a bowl like that he demonstrates.
I use one of them clip-ons says another boldly.
The lady probation officer interrupts
Uh-huh, you still need to learn how to tie a tie.
When I recite the Hayden poem they won't look up.

Rondeau

I love the profile picture on your page.
You look so young I'd swear you're underage.
I'll get right to the point and ask you why
my friend request did not get a reply.
Why is it that you chose to disengage

from me? Like looking at an unused stage,
at night, I stare into your empty wall, engage
in fantasies. Will you accept, deny?
I love the profile picture on your page.

Without a sign, an instrument to gauge
what's going on, don't even know what age
your children are! I do not mean to pry.
O no, you must believe that's not a lie.
Repeat, *deep breath*, do not succumb to rage.
I love the profile picture on your page.

Running With Isabel

My parents sit behind a folding table,
red one with the gold flecked top,

black metal legs. The table
I looked up at when they played bridge,
after dusk, before they put me to bed.

Acrid scent
of ashes, bright red rings around
the ladies' stubs, and the sweetness of the scotch

against the salt of those papery skins in the peanut dish.
I can almost smudge the impression
of their lips pressed into a cocktail glass.

So unlike this place where I ended up,
today, at dusk, the parking lot beams tinged blue,
boys at soccer behind a chain link fence,

a father tossing a baseball
too small to see,
where I run with my 6 year old daughter
across the clumps of outfield grass, to a place

chosen randomly, soccer goal
against a fence, and can't stop running

up against what I expect to see,
and what is no longer there:
my hand in front of hers,
about to touch the rusty pole.

Sea Turtle

How often did I navigate the ladder rails
attuned only to the touch of my palms,
and the balance required to make a calm
maneuver to the grated landing? I'd bail
the contents of my bag: the razors, mail,
the clippers, magazines, Tiger balm,
to sort them on my bed that Fall
in mid-Pacific (a diversion that never failed
to pass an empty hour). I shopped alone.
How charming then when a turtle appeared
one day beside the hull, below the wall
of gauzy turquoise sea, an emerald stone
etched in armored facets, a leathery sphere
like a fortune rising in an eight ball.

Somebody Threw A Big Rock Through The Window

The curb's cracked blush prevented parking.
The water meter said: "Open up."
Christ lit up a cigarette on the bus-stop
and stroked his beard.
Walt Whitman asked him:
"How was the weather in Paso Robles?"
"The sky was like a neon notary,"
he replied.   Cesar said: "The stars
felt like snowflakes and the trees looked
the way blackberries taste."
Small towns define themselves
by their curb trees.
Christ and Walt Whitman
spoke to no one in particular.
Then: "somebody threw a big rock
through the window."
"I know." The two-way glass shattered.
The red brick of certainty
will not distract anyone here for long.

The Stocking Cap

Only 12 years old,
I parted my hair;
a thin, white line
of scalp appeared
between the dark waves
that curled out
like the wake turbulence
off a jet's wing.

That night, in front of
the bathroom mirror,
I worked the white Brylcreem
over the ends
that wouldn't lie straight:
foaming, querulous kinks.

The combing done,
I tied a knot in the loose flap
of my mother's nylon
and slid my little cap
over my head, tucking in
the offending hair.

Ready for bed, I stared
as an acolyte, robed
before the altar, might
raise the host to the priest
and wait, hands at his side,
for transubstantiation.

Sympathetic Nervous System

I'm sitting in this plane; I haven't slept.
I'm slumped down in my seat, a bit on edge.
Some unexpected turbulence is dredging
up a shot of pure adrenaline. Unkempt.
My hair is greasy. Three hours in I wept
for who knows who or why. My pledge
was to be stoical. Instead, I'm wedged
between a serving tray and dread. "Accept-
ing what I cannot change" ain't happenin.'
Some tremors riff across the ginger ale.
I'm flying into forces I can't see
but only sense. It's a prevailing wind
that rattles on the wing and makes me pale
that pulls from underneath me suddenly.

The Tao

I drove my car to Santa Rita jail
and on the way I couldn't help but think
that this collage of images will with a blink
evaporate. In just a year this pale
façade will pixelate, memory fail
to bind the dots. This pool will slowly sink
into a vat, a dead computer link,
no longer needed, undelivered mail.
What will remain is what I'm feeling now,
the rising and the falling of my chest,
the hum that's undefined inside my ear,
perhaps a drop of thankfulness. The Tao
repeats: count syllables, which beat is stressed?
It's not the words, it's what you hear.

Tiger Stadium 1968

Beyond the concrete steps, below the decks,
between the girders, rows of wooden seats
pattern, hinged, unhinged; a ball and bat connects,
and hatched crossed the infield grass, the cleats
of Donald Wert are turning, glinting. Clay
turns up in mounds where he has worked. The bag
at third so bleached it's almost blue. Parquet
cuts of lawn crowd the groundskeepers who drag
the diamond. Is this the rabbit hole?
Before I sit, I scan the rows
of rickety green chairs, absorb this view
of men at ruthless play. This place a bowl
of designs, at twelve, but dimly perceived, a tableau
to parse, a place to keep score of what ensues.

Tornados

I only saw them on a TV show—
domesticated funnels that lifted up
a sculpted model or an animated bungalow
in which a saucer and a coffee cup
might be floating near a reading lamp,
where Mickey folds his evening paper.
His swirling, yellow pulp of damp
gazette dissolves into recording tape.

Above the asphalt, where the reflected dome
of sky dismissed our class from school
and instructed us to run directly home;
the silence, like a movie reel, unspooled.
At night, in bed, I listened by the radio
to descriptions of what I could not know.

The Tower Of Skulls

1

On a screen at the Naval seminar
a tower rises like an enormous kiln,
a smokestack, from the town of Nis.
Built in the Serb's last stronghold,
a talismanic warning, our lesson:
the Turks embedded the inner walls
with the chalky skulls of Serbs.
Some still stare into the center,
surrounded only by themselves.
Cool bones. Nothing remains
of their human heads
except the sockets,
the empty spaces in the wall--
the marks chiseled out by a sister, or a mother.

2

Perhaps he found it at an auction
lying on its side.
The eye holes stare back.
The porous snout rusted open
on its hinge. An iron mask.
The African American, a collector,
points for the camera:
"A plate keeps down the tongue
so that nothing may be swallowed or eaten,
not even saliva,
a passage for which is made through holes.
When long worn it becomes so heated
as frequently to bring off the skin."
He holds it up in his hands.

Tree Frog

She said it's time you wrote your exercise
about the frog who came out of a tree
and ate his way into an orange twice his size.

I told her right off that I despise
poets who write about the trivial or with fatuity.
She said, "It's time you did your exercise."

I told her I tried to, that I prefer to agonize
over a tragedy, a victim or an amputee,
not a frog who ate his way into an orange twice his size.

It's more in my nature to elegize
a girl who's captured like Persephone.
She said it's time you wrote your exercise.

I tried: We have a friend who will, surely, metastasize,
And I wrote about our psychotherapy.
It's time, she said, you did your exercise
before the frog eats his way into an orange twice his size.

Triolet

The muse is driving down the interstate.
I try to call her cell; she won't pick up.
I leave my name, the time, the date.
The muse is driving down the interstate.
She won't return my calls, it's getting late.
She passes on the right but won't look up.
The muse is driving down the Interstate.
I try to call her cell; she won't pick up.

Villanelle

(Spielberg visited an inner city school in response to a class of black students who had laughed inappropriately at a showing of his movie about the holocaust Schindler's List.)

When Steven spoke at Oakland High
A custodian swept up the shattered glass,
replaced the broken clocks to satisfy

the Governor, who was preoccupied
with becoming President, with covering his ass
When Steven Spielberg spoke at Oakland High

the District found diminishing supplies
of disinfectant and toilet paper stashed
away, so they replaced the clocks instead to satisfy

the cameras and the press that they had rectified
the deficiencies among the underclass.
When Steven Spielberg spoke at Oakland High

the students didn't seem dissatisfied
about the cover up, just happy to be out of class.
The custodian replaced the broken clocks to satisfy

this need we have to falsify
the truth in subservience to cash.
When Steven Spielberg came to Oakland High
the custodian replaced the broken clocks.

What Nationality Are You

the pleasant, young blond woman in the flowered
brocade dress and pumps wants to know in 1965.
Prepared by my parents
I tell this adult that I'm American
and watch her slightly exaggerated smile
droop and her attractive forehead
wrinkle. *What I meant was what ethnicity…*
she attempts, but that particular word,
that multiplicity of syllables
congeals on her lip gloss like
an oil slick. An electric charge
of embarrassment surges
through us like the experiment
in class when we all linked hands
while the teacher cranked
the coiled generator.

When I Heard About Troy Davis

Distract myself or meditate, to divide
my life into impermeable zones
to keep me from imagining when I'm alone
what the radio report repeats: he died.
It was a shock, as though a friend had died,
as though I were waiting by the phone;
to hear the news, the news I've known
would come but pretended wouldn't. I've tried.

Outside the wall a klieg, a talking head
in ghastly light, a skeleton on stilts
collect. A frazzled prison guard complains
to dreadlocked kids who trample on his bed
of bulbs. A battle group of nuns tilt
into the crowd the barricade restrains.

Where You Lie

Stopped mid-sentence
exhausted by words,
not willing to risk another,
I stare where you lie
in the broken field of our bed.
One leg is cocked up
like a question mark,
or a trigger finger.
Your arms triangulate
into a tumble of hair.
I tighten the loops in my tie.
Slowly, you slide your hips forward
and I choose to see a large bruise
on the underside of your thigh.
Its tender, purple center
spills yellow, blooms.

About the Author

George Higgins, born in Detroit, Michigan, is a public defender in Oakland, California. He received a J.D. from the University of Michigan Law School where he studied with Robert Hayden and an M.F.A. from Warren Wilson College where he was a Holden Fellow. His first published poem, a villanelle, was selected for Best American Poetry 2003 by Yusef Komunyakaa. Other poems have appeared in Fugue, Lungfull, Nimrod, Pleiades, and Salamander. George is presently a Cave Canem Fellow. He lives in Oakland with his wife Sharon and his dog Puck. This is his first book.

Made in the USA
Las Vegas, NV
12 December 2020